Affiliate Marketing

Beginners' Comprehensive Guide To Choosing The Best Affiliate Programs

(Affiliate Marketing Success Unlocking The Code)

Gianbattista Pasquini

TABLE OF CONTENT

Introduction 1

Chapter 1: What Can You Expect To Find In This Book?.. 4

Chapter 2: What Is An Affiliate Program?..................... 8

Chapter 3: Affiliate Marketing Vocabulary 10

Chapter 4: Content That Sells 36

Chapter 5: The Methods For Starting Out 40

Chapter 6: How To Choose A Product With Minimal Rivalry And High Demand 49

Chapter 7: How To Launch An Affiliate Marketing Campaign 58

Chapter 8: How To Write An Email 62

Chapter 9: Making Money Through Advertising 68

Chapter 10: Affiliate Marketing Comprehensively. 72

Chapter 11: Ppc Marketing And Other Promotional Methods 77

Chapter 12: The Idea Behind Drop Shipping 93

Chapter 13: What Is Dropshipping 97

Chapter 14: Real-World Examples Of Superb Affiliate Marketing Success 114

Chapter 15: Some Certain Methods To Immediately Boost Your Affiliate Income 119

Introduction

The methods and strategies for conducting business are always evolving. The world of marketing is comparable to a vast ocean in which every drip of creativity and innovation easily becomes diluted. In lieu of promoting their products or services, individuals have been using antiquated methods of incentivizing others. Now, the digital realm has expanded the purview of conducting business. The introduction of the internet and internet-enabled devices has altered the mentality of people, who have become extremely communicative. Thus, both the area and volume of business have expanded exponentially.

Digital marketing is an umbrella term for a collection of services that generate marketing opportunities for users. For the promotion of their brand, people are no longer reliant solely on conventional and costly advertising methods. We are soaring through the aviation age, and the internet has permeated our lives. Why not utilize the available resources to conduct business with a unique but effective strategy?

Digital marketing enables users to engage in promotional activities via the internet, social media networking sites, webpages, blogs, smartphones, and search engines. Digital marketing has become a prevalent trend, with an increasing number of businesses utilizing it to promote their brands. Digital marketing's essential objective is the collection of internet-enabled devices and appliances used to promote brands. These methods are also utilized by digital entrepreneurs to introduce their products and services to the market. Do you understand what digital entrepreneur means?

The methods of conducting business in the era of technology characterized by digitalization differ from the traditional method. The purpose of business has always been to generate profits. The numerous technological tools have enabled people to earn offline and online. Why not maximize the available resources and attempt to improve the standard of living? An additional source of income will aid in paying expenses, managing groceries, paying rent, taking dream vacations, and living life to the fullest.

Chapter 1: What Can You Expect To Find In This Book?

This book aims to familiarize readers with digital business practices. If you delve deeply into the topic, you will discover a plethora of digitalization-based online business expansion strategies. Entrepreneurs in the digital age aspire to reach a global audience because they have expanded their horizons by taking their businesses online.

Human-like duties performed by machines, such as computers, are becoming increasingly common. Computers' problem-solving techniques are commonly referred to as artificial intelligence (AI) in layman's terms. Let me simplify the situation for you.

You should be familiar with Siri, Alexa, Cortana, and Google Assistant. Who is this? It consists of digital voice assistants. This is one of the simplest examples of AI, and the reason I've included it here is because we use them frequently in our daily lives.

A mechanism that functions like a human brain is a marvelous example of advanced technology. AI is the discipline concerned with such machines. As its name suggests, artificial intelligence is the simulation of the human intellect through machines and computers to make decisions and solve problems. AI tools are created by humans to complete tasks that have been predetermined and defined by the human intellect. AI tools are increasingly incorporated into business models of all sizes. From the manufacturing stage in industries to customer service interactions, it is straightforward to identify the use of AI-assisted tools. Websites, blogs, and social media networking sites serve as the online platforms for product and service promotion.

The greatest boon that the digital world has bestowed upon humanity is the ability to generate passive income from the convenience of one's own home. If you have a smartphone, computer, or laptop with an internet connection, you can begin working from home immediately.

Affiliate marketing is another essential term that you will learn in this book. It is one of the most prevalent formats for passive income generation. Affiliate marketing is a model of advertising in which a company pays a commission to an individual (affiliate) or third-party publisher for generating leads or traffic for the company's services or products. The affiliate's commission serves as an incentive offered by the company for promoting its products or services.

How does the book assist readers?

Anyone interested in affiliate marketing as a source of passive income will find this book fascinating. Indulging in such an activity is not only fascinating, but it also yields tangible benefits.

But let's not undervalue the power of AI-based affiliate marketing as a passive income source. The concept as a whole can replace the full-time employment model for readers if it is executed correctly and with strategic planning. As we reside in the digital age, we cannot ignore the significance of digital tools and devices in our daily existence. It is reasonable to presume that affiliate marketing has the potential to become a stable income model for users, given that our reliance on such devices is growing by the day.

So, let us immediately begin reading the book.

Chapter 2: What Is An Affiliate Program?

Affiliate marketing is a model of advertising in which a business compensates third-party promoters for generating traffic or leads for its products and services. External distributors are subsidiaries, and the commission fee encourages them to seek out opportunities to advance the organization.

Partner advertising may not be a form of advertising you're familiar with, as it differs from the majority of subsidiary advertising's fundamentals.Differentiating factor is the inclusion of outsiders to generate leads and changes.

In the past five years, the industry for subsidiary marketing has nearly multiplied, demonstrating dramatic growth. It is a low-to-no-cost endeavor that can yield enormous returns, and it is acceptable, scalable, and straightforward to implement. This method's numerous advantages have led to it becoming one of the most popular modern advertising strategies.

All organizations utilizing the methodology profit from affiliate marketing. If you are considering it as a part-time employment, you may end up driving more traffic to your website or blog. Assuming you are the organization executing it, you can profit from additional sales and modifications while growing your audience.

Chapter 3: Affiliate Marketing Vocabulary

Occasionally, an affiliate link is also referred to as a referral link or an affiliate ID. When you join up as an affiliate for a product or service, your unique affiliate link distinguishes you from other affiliates. This is essential, given that some affiliate networks contain hundreds of affiliates.

The vendor must be able to attribute a purchase to you. Using a unique affiliate link is the optimal approach for doing so. Typically, an affiliate program registration requires a unique logon. This information is then appended to your affiliate links.

Your unique affiliate link is essential to earning commissions. You don't want to devote a great deal of time and energy to promoting a business or service, only to have your sales attributed to another affiliate! You can now duplicate your affiliate link directly from affiliate networks and programs. Use caution when employing this.

Affiliate Supply

A specific product or service that you can market in exchange for a commission constitutes an affiliate offer. The majority of affiliate networks publish a list of their available affiliate offers alongside vital statistics such as sales volume and conversion rates, as well as other information.

Typically, you will have access to a unique affiliate link for each affiliate offer. When a visitor clicks on this link, they will be directed to the sales portal for the product or service, and you will receive credit. You will receive commissions on any sales generated by your referrals.

Affiliate System

An affiliate network is a website that provides you access to various affiliate offers. One of the most well-known affiliate networks, Clickbank.com may provide you with access to hundreds of exclusive affiliate offers.

The majority of affiliate networks will provide you with essential data regarding their affiliate offerings. In most cases, information regarding a product or service's popularity, conversion rate, potential commission, and other factors is readily available.

Affiliate networks bring together vendors of products and services and affiliates. If they do not already have their own affiliate program, a vendor will use an affiliate network to inform affiliates about their products. Some affiliate networks permit the marketing of products and services automatically. Others will require you to obtain approval from specific product vendors.

Affiliate Director

On some affiliate networks, specialized affiliate administrators are available to support your success. By using email or instant messaging, they can communicate directly with you. Staying in contact with your affiliate manager will help you determine which affiliate offers will generate the highest conversions.

Average Order Value

The affiliate network will reveal the average order value for each affiliate offer. Numerous products and services offer enhancements so that consumers can enhance their purchases.

These upsells will be included in the calculation of the average order value. The average amount spent by customers on a particular product will be displayed. This is essential, as you will typically earn commissions on both initial purchases and enhancements.

Bonuses

You will have an advantage in affiliate marketing, which can be highly competitive, if you can provide clients with connected benefits that other affiliates cannot. In the areas of making money online and Internet marketing, incentives are commonly offered.

If you are promoting an affiliate product that explains how to develop an email list and sell to it, you could offer your own email swipes as a bonus. You've utilized these communications in the past, and they have a high conversion rate. Customers will use your affiliate link to make purchases if they believe you offer the best incentives; in this case, you will earn a commission.

CTR (Click-Through Rate)

The click-through rate (CTR) is an essential metric that measures the number of visits on your affiliate offer link. It is expressed as a percentage based on the number of impressions your link receives. If you can achieve a high CTR, your chances of earning more commissions will increase.

Consider that you have 10,000 email list subscribers. The email containing your affiliate link is opened by 5,000 of your subscribers. This means that 5,000 individuals have viewed your link. If 500 of your subscribers follow the link, your CTR is 10%.

Conversion Effort

This is yet another significant indicator. Using the click-through rate example from earlier, you direct 500 people to the affiliate offer you are promoting. Your conversion rate depends on the number of consumers who actually make a purchase.

Consequently, your conversion rate is 10% if 50 out of 500 consumers complete a purchase. Similar to click-through rates, conversion rates should be as high as possible. Affiliates can experiment with the conversion rates of various offers. They may employ sponsored traffic to determine how many of their views result in sales. If the conversion rate is high, businesses may invest in additional traffic to increase revenue.

Cookies

A cookie is a piece of code that is used to identify a user who has clicked on one of your affiliate links. Typically, the affiliate program or network will identify cookies for a specified time period and use them for surveillance purposes.

Let's presume that the cookie term for your promotion is 30 days. This means that if a visitor returns to the product or service's sales page within the specified time frame, the affiliate who initially referred them will be credited with the sale and receive the commission.

CPA - Cost Per Action

Affiliates are paid commissions in cost-per-action (CPA) marketing when a visitor clicks on their affiliate link and completes a specified task. This may include providing their email address, answering a few simple inquiries, providing their zip code, etc.

CPA offerings are popular among affiliate marketers because they do not require a transaction to earn a commission. Since the visitor is not required to make a purchase, the conversion rates of CPA offers are typically much higher. Nevertheless, commission rates for CPA proposals are typically lower than for closing transactions.

CPL (Cost Per Lead)

Cost-per-lead (CPL) advertising typically requires a visitor to submit their email address, call a specified phone number, or provide some other contact information for the advertiser. A CPL offer does not require a sale for an affiliate marketer to earn a commission.

CPS (Cost Per Sale)

CPS offers are the most popular form of affiliate offer. Affiliates receive an agreed-upon commission for each visitor they refer who makes a purchase. CPS products typically have higher commission rates than CPA and CPL products. However, this is not always the case; therefore, research is required.

Data Feeds

Certain affiliate networks and programs may provide affiliates with a data feed for use on their websites. It is a file containing information about the products and services an advertiser provides, such as:

Names of products and services

The price of the merchandise or services

Images of merchandise or services

Descriptions

Unique affiliate connections

Affiliates may use this data stream to display the entire product line on their website. If a visitor clicks on the affiliate link in the data feed to learn more and then makes a purchase, the affiliate will receive a commission.

Earnings Per Click (EPC) is another important metric you must be aware of. The affiliate network or program may provide EPC data for all of its products and services. An EPC is a monetary representation of the commission amount that each affiliate will receive for each click on their affiliate link, for example $10.

Impressions

Impressions indicate the frequency with which your advertisement or affiliate link is displayed. Some websites charge for advertising on the premise of "cost per thousand impressions" (CPM). One of your email marketing impressions is the number of times a subscriber opens an email and views your affiliate link.

Landing Page

When a user selects on one of your links, they are redirected to a landing page. This link may lead you directly to the product or service's sales page. Instead of simply linking their visitors to a sales page, shrewd affiliate marketers are increasingly directing them to their own landing pages.

Obtaining the visitor's email address is one of the primary purposes of this action. Once you have a customer's email address, you can immediately direct them to the vendor's sales page. You can utilize either a landing page or a bridge page to prepare your visitor for the vendor sales page.

Many advertising networks prohibit sending consumers to a sales page. Google and Facebook will require that you create an instructional landing page. You may then choose where to dispatch the visitor.

If you want to be successful as an affiliate marketer, you must focus on both inquiries and sales. Utilizing a landing page that requests the visitor's email address enables you to generate a valuable lead that you can contact again. Some of the prospects may make purchases through your affiliate link, thereby increasing your earnings.

Email leads are vital because you can communicate with your visitors at any time. If you simply send a visitor to a vendor's sales page, you run the risk of losing them permanently if they do not make a purchase. Not everyone will purchase an item the first time it goes on sale. Having email prospects allows you to contact them again directly.

Niche Markets

The most effective affiliate marketers focus on specific niche markets. They create a website, blog, YouTube channel, or other affiliate channels centered on their chosen topic, and they use content to add value for their visitors. The promotion of affiliate products tailored to a specific market niche may generate commissions.

Choosing the proper market segment is crucial. You must ensure that the niche has a sufficient market size and is profitable. The most popular markets where profits are assuredly generated include: - Wealth creation

- Health and fitness (such as weight loss)

- Self-development

These markets are in perpetual demand. In these three categories, numerous affiliate programs exist. Nonetheless, because of their high levels of competition, it is prudent to seek out other lucrative industries. Combine keyword research with methods of demonstrating that money is being exchanged in the niche (are affiliate offers available) to determine demand.

Pay Per Click (PPC) describes a circumstance in which an advertiser pays a sum of money to the website hosting the advertisement when a user clicks on the advertisement. Google and Bing are frequently regarded as the finest search engines for PPC. This is because users enter a specific search phrase (keyword) to locate the information they seek. As an affiliate, you may purchase PPC traffic from Google or Microsoft in order to attract interested customers to your offers.

Once quite affordable, the price of pay-per-click (PPC) traffic has increased substantially over time. Traffic from Microsoft sites such as Bing and MSN is typically less expensive than Google PPC. Paid traffic is an excellent method for evaluating conversion rates for offers, as you can typically begin receiving targeted visitors within minutes.

After creating the tutorial, you want as many people as possible to view it. Remember that quality content is desired. If your audience is engaged and enthusiastic, they will return to your site more frequently and remain longer.

It is essential to keep in mind the quality rule when selecting products. Many bloggers do not appear to select their products based on quality. They promote everything. On occasion, they may be promoting quality products, but they don't appear to care how they promote them. They never employ a novel method of product promotion. You should carefully evaluate the vendor. They value their consumers and their reputation. The poor promotion of their products does not enhance their reputation.

This is one reason why video tutorials are so popular. They provide a fresh perspective on an old product or a first glimpse at a new one. When you provide valuable content to your audience, you help to establish their trust.

Social media — If you're searching for a medium that helps you connect with a large audience, social media is it. All affiliate marketers must reach out to a large number of individuals. Social media sites can help you do it. Affiliate marketers can utilize social media as a potent instrument. Social media websites such as Facebook, LinkedIn, and Twitter allow you to connect with individuals from various backgrounds and share your thoughts with them.

There are a number of ways in which social media can contribute to the success of your affiliate marketing strategy. They consist of:

• Promotion of the affiliate programs - Once you've built a following, your friends will be able to share your posts and links. You can advertise the products for which you are an affiliate on your page through posts and blogs. Additionally, fan pages can be created, which will enhance your promotion.

• Establish rapport with your audience — You can expand your network of contacts by adding individuals who will value what you have to say. By creating interactive groups, coordination with your audience will be enhanced. After providing the audience with information about your affiliate products, solicit their feedback. In addition to fostering rapport with your audience, feedback can help you make necessary adjustments to your strategy. Inform them of your affiliate products and solicit their feedback.

• Remain current - You'll want to be aware of what's happening in your market area. Through social media, you can learn about all new product launches and which ones the public appears to favor the most. This will assist you in understanding current trends and adjusting your affiliate marketing strategies accordingly.

Due to the fact that you will not be the only affiliate marketer, there is substantial competition for success with your strategy. Here are a few strategies to help you gain a competitive edge on social media sites:

• Focus on relationships — Social media sites include Facebook, Google+, and Twitter. There, the keyword is "social." Ensure that you communicate with the appropriate individuals and develop a positive rapport with them. Try having an infinite number of follower pages.

This will assist you gain additional knowledge. Developing a solid relationship with prospective consumers will aid in marketing. They will want to share your content with their Facebook peers.

• Include social bookmarking—You can add a bookmarking icon to your website. Then, request that your visitors follow. This makes it simple for people to share your posts if they enjoy them. Utilize social bookmarking without incurring any costs.

• Blog smarter...not harder—Some bloggers exert great effort and devote countless hours preparing blogs that are rarely read. When creating blog posts for your website, blog intelligently. The primary objective should be to attract the visitor's attention. Provide them with valuable, informative, and specific information once you have done so. Your social media presence will increase if you take this action.

Improving your web presence is essential, and these tips will assist you in doing so. Once you have a solid understanding of social media, it will be simpler to locate and connect with prospective clients. Once you've selected the appropriate products/services to promote, you should be straightforward with your prospective consumers. You can win their affections through social media if you do so.

Email list—The majority of bloggers do not use email marketing because they do not believe they can profit from it. They fail to recognize the benefits. They simply believe it is not worth their effort, so they do not attempt it. Like a new restaurant, if you don't experience it, you won't know what it's like. You might be missing out on something exceptional.

As a blogger, there are a number of considerations you must not neglect, as doing so will prove to be a mistake. Before you commence your email marketing campaign, there are a few things you should be aware of.

• Develop your subscriber list - You want as many subscribers as possible on your list. If your email were a blog, it would receive traffic. Your email marketing subscribers represent your traffic. The greater the blog's traffic, the better the results. The same applies to email and subscribers. More resources produce greater results.

• Be original — Numerous users of email marketing fail to be original in their communications. This is one of the most effective methods for converting subscribers to unsubscribers. People will immediately unsubscribe if they believe your communications do not contain original, valuable content. They do not want their inbox to be filled with spam.

• Write to demonstrate your familiarity with the product you're promoting — There is nothing worse than a "canned" review derived directly from advertising copy. Readers want to believe that you understand what you're discussing. They seek a personal touch that demonstrates product knowledge. If possible, you should request the item and use it first. This provides you with firsthand knowledge to share with your audience. Thus, you will be in a better position to answer any concerns your readers may have about the products.

• Write sincere evaluations; not every product you evaluate will be "awesome." Some will just be "average." Whatever the matter may be, state it clearly. You can give your reviews a straightforward number rating like 1—2—3—4—5. However, be sure to offer it the rating you believe it deserves.

9. Create a focused distribution list

Building a targeted mailing list is one of the most essential things you can do to achieve success with affiliate marketing. This will enable you to maintain contact with your prospective clients and keep them informed of your most recent offerings.

When constructing a mailing list, there are several factors to consider:

- Ensure you have a clear understanding of your intended audience. This will assist you in determining what content to include in your messages.

- Keep your communications brief and to the point. No one is interested in reading a novel written by an affiliate marketer!

Include a compelling call to action in each message. This could read, "Click here to learn more about our latest product!"

- Make it simple for individuals to unsubscribe from your mailing list if they no longer wish to receive your communications.

By following these guidelines, you will be well on your way to creating a successful mailing list for affiliate marketing.

• Who currently serves this audience?

When you have identified a potential niche audience, it is often beneficial to examine your competitors. Is it viable if there is no competition in this market sector? Some may advise you to choose markets with less competition, but if your conversion rate is in line with industry norms, it's best to choose a market with enough potential customers to help you reach your income goals.

If there are 1,000 potential customers, they convert at a rate of 4 to 7 percent, and you know you can get your materials and information in front of them, you may obtain, for example, 70 clients through a campaign. At your current pricing point, are these 70 customers enough to generate a profit?

What expertise and products do you have to offer this market?

Because of your education, background, or expertise, are you uniquely qualified for this specialization? To be successful in a niche, you need not be a member of the target market.

For example, even if you have no prior experience with camping or enthusiasm for it, you can still learn about it and benefit your audience if you have identified a niche that requires guidance on how to use unique camping gear that is not currently available. Instead of gaining direct experience, you could use your financial resources to hire industry experts to assist you in establishing your business.

- What Makes You Unique?

Always keep your actions in mind. What distinguishes you from your competitors? What unique abilities can you bring to this market? How can you distinguish yourself from others? Will you approach the niche differently than others? As a business coach, for instance, are you formal or informal? Regardless of who you are, you will always attract a wholly different fan base than someone who is not like you.

• Search for products in a network of affiliates that serves that market.

Ensure that your topic is profitable as your second priority. It is essential to consider whether it will be profitable. An online pastime does not always translate into a profitable niche. Profitable when the target market is large enough and has the means to pay for the products and services produced and provided.

Once you have narrowed down your options, the most essential factors to consider are whether or not your niche idea is profitable and whether or not you possess the necessary skills - either those you can learn or those you can purchase from others. Choose a market niche that you are qualified to serve, that you are interested in, and that has the potential to generate a substantial profit.

Now that you have determined your target market and the market niche you wish to operate in, you must select the ideal products and/or services to offer them. There are multiple ways to discover the products or services to offer consumers.

Chapter 4: Content That Sells

Creating viral content is crucial, but you must also recognize that likable content is not necessarily content that converts. It can be quite easy to build an audience that enjoys your posts. However, growing a customer base that feels compelled to purchase from you can be considerably more difficult.

Your marketing strategy should include three categories of content that support the three stages of a sales funnel: content that is likable, content that builds relationships, and sales content.

Likable Content

Likable content consists of everything in the preceding chapter's category. In other words, content created with the intention of being found. This content may not always go viral, but it is more likely to be viewed by new audience members and get you discovered by the appropriate individuals.

Relationship-Developing Material

After landing on your page, visitors must develop a relationship with you. This content is less likely to receive as many likes and shares as your appealing content, but it will attract those who are most interested in you. Consequently, they will develop an affinity for your brand.

Relationship-building content includes content that: - Shares your business's history - Describes why you are impassioned about your business - Demonstrates who you are

It could be behind-the-scenes content, an introduction post, or any other content that provides a more personal glimpse into your brand.

Sales Content

In conclusion, sales content is a crucial component of your conversion strategy. This is content that is intended to persuade readers to buy something. Use sales content sparingly to maintain its effectiveness. It will work most effectively if you have spent sufficient time cultivating relationships with your audience, so that they have confidence in you and are willing to trust your sales content.

Your sales content should offer superficially similar categories of content to your likable and relationship-building content. For instance, displaying behind-the-scenes or adhering to a specific trend. Aside from that, it should include numerous call-to-actions (CTAs) to encourage users to do more than like, remark, and share. The call to action should direct people to your website, your direct messages, or wherever else they must go to purchase the product or service you are selling.

Chapter 5: The Methods For Starting Out

A highly profitable endeavor begins with research and planning. Utilize this getting started checklist to help you truly get prepared and take the first step toward affiliate marketing profits.

Determine Your Audience — Conduct research to gain as much knowledge as possible in order to become viable options for them.marketing graph based on every product, service, and problem that your audience has because it wants to communicate with the target audience in such a way that they comprehend what set up branded social Platforms — The same applies to your social media platforms; do they enjoy receiving information from them? information to notify them regarding the matter. Do not give up if you initially fail; consider your audience. Where do they seek refuge? What causes them to lose sleep? Who the audience is and why you are the best person to discover or create the product are the foundation of your email.

Autoresponder — You cannot achieve success without email marketing, so start building your list with gifts before you have any products.

Become an affiliate for that product — Register as an affiliate if you can identify the need to be branded appropriately so that everyone knows it's you. Every product that you will be promoting to them.

A Manual for Locating and Promoting Affiliate Products

Okay, enough with the conjecture; how does one get started as an affiliate marketer? An item is the initial action. To purchase this item, you must visit an online retailer such as Clickbank or Commission Junction. JVZoo is similarly beneficial. Here are numerous affiliate programs, allowing you to choose from a variety of products. You can browse down until something of interest appears. Utilize the available information about the various products to your advantage by selecting those that sell well and pay a reasonable commission. When a website provides a rough estimate of sales, it is useful to seek out products that are selling in large quantities. Once you have chosen a product to market, it is necessary to contact the company behind it. If accepted, you will be provided with a unique URL that you may use as you see appropriate. Consider that many affiliate products will include promotional materials. Remember that God is also prospering alongside you. They have a vested interest in your success and frequently provide promotional tools such as emails, a sales website, banner advertisements, and more. If you're just starting out in the business world, I recommend selecting a product with these additional features. Copy and paste the extant materials into your new endeavor, and you will be up and running in no time. Since you'll be using the same product and proposal, there is no reason you shouldn't achieve comparable sales success.

As stated previously, this is a "copy-and-paste" business strategy. If a product is already performing well on the market due to a well-established system, all you need to do to compete is implement the system and direct the profits to your bank account. Selling Goods and Services for a Profit Although selling eBooks on marketplaces such as JVZoo is a great way to maximize profits, these sites do have disadvantages. Despite what other sellers may attempt to persuade you of, tangible products continue to be the most sought-after online. This makes complete sense if you give it some thought. How well do you know individuals who prefer to acquire physical items? Do you all or nearly all concur? However, what percentage of your peers and family would purchase an ebook? Unless you give your grandmother a Kindle, she probably won't be able to read a PDF file if she doesn't know how to open one. A friend who does not share your passion for literature would also not share it. That indicates you have a substantially smaller market share. As an affiliate marketer, the question now is how to go about selling physical products. Become an Amazon Associate is the most popular option.

Many advertisers are enticed by Amazon's associate scheme, which operates similarly to an affiliate program but is managed by Amazon itself. When researching affiliate marketing, the majority of the content you find will focus on promoting and selling digital products via marketplaces such as JVZoo, ClickBank, and Commission Junction. Things are not as they appear on Amazon. To generate a respectable profit, you will need to sell a large quantity of items at significantly higher prices. Therefore, is it necessary that you not contemplate working with Amazon Associates? The contrary is true. First, the margins on physical product sales are frequently significantly higher than those on digital product sales. Consider: would you rather spend a lot of money on a product that you can hold in your hands and show off to your peers, or on a product that you must view on a screen? Customers recognize and respect Amazon as a brand and company. This increases customer propensity to purchase, and it only requires one click!

When selling on Amazon, you can choose from a vast selection of items, so there is sure to be something suitable for every item you post. Lastly, you will still receive compensation if a consumer visits Amazon via your link but purchases a different product. For example, if someone purchased a new computer and you received 8% of that amount, it could amount to a significant sum of money. As long as the customer is brought to Amazon in the first place, indirect product promotion is still eligible for commission. What then is the best course of action? Employ both types of affiliate marketing! However, do not overlook Amazon, or you will lose out. In subsequent chapters, you will learn alternative strategies for advertising Amazon products to generate the most revenue. (Note: If you do not live in the same country as Amazon, there is a restriction on how you can earn money through Amazon Associates. Thus, if you are a business based in the United Kingdom, you should direct them to Amazon UK. You can still sell on Amazon.com, but you will only receive coupons in exchange for your efforts.

Alternative Trade Channels for Tangible Goods Amazon dominates the online market for physical products, but they are not the only game in town. Numerous brands even offer affiliate networks for online merchants. the number of brick-and-mortar retailers is astounding. If you search for additional items, you may discover one that is more closely associated with the theme of your website. To locate pertinent affiliate programs, try searching Google with "affiliate program + your niche." Additionally, a number of online resources list the best affiliate programs for a variety of fields. If the retailer or manufacturer you're targeting does not have an affiliate program, you may also... in addition to requesting that they create one for you. If successful, you may be able to negotiate an exclusive arrangement as well as a hefty commission. Obviously, if you want this to be successful, you will need to demonstrate that you have sufficient influence to warrant their investment.

You could also endeavor to sell a service or SAAS. This path may result in the most remarkable earnings. This is because a significant proportion of services offer recurring revenue sharing. Suppose you have convinced someone to create an online casino account. In certain online casinos, the affiliate program will pay a percentage of the player's future winnings for as long as they remain brand customers. Similarly, assume you can convince a person to subscribe to a hosting account or recurring service. Initially, the commission will logically be modest. However, this period may ultimately add up to a considerable sum. If you are able to establish a large enough subscriber base over several years, you can continue to receive payments even if you are forced to close your website.

Chapter 6: How To Choose A Product With Minimal Rivalry And High Demand

When searching for an evergreen product to sell, whether physical, digital, service, or software, market demand should be your primary concern. Throughout your business voyage, market demand is crucial, and when there is no demand for a particular product, there is no need to promote it.

If you know how to conduct marketing research, you will discover an evergreen product that is uncontested and has a high search volume.

How do you locate these items? To locate the most desirable products with minimal competition and high search volume. Before researching your competition, you must first investigate the market's demand. I'll share some tips on the most effective way to locate those products to sell.

Solve problems with your products.

Numerous consumers desire products that aid in problem-solving, and the market demand for these products is extremely high. However, the rate at which you can repeatedly sell the same product depends on your marketing strategies.

For example, the majority of marketing professionals can spend thousands of dollars on a single product to generate passive income, and they employ their marketing strategies to sell expensive products. They can easily persuade or influence individuals to become paying customers.

Since you are a complete beginner, your product marketing strategies are distinct and your budget is limited, so low-priced products will be productive for you. Using the checklist discussed in the previous section, you can readily identify these products on the Amazon marketplace.

Why are these items essential?

Before you begin selling a product, you must ensure that it is in demand and continually validate and verify it to ensure that it will generate revenue. This implies that no product should be promoted if it does not provide positive responses to these criteria. This saves you additional time, money, and assets.

While conducting investigation on the product you intend to sell, you must also test out other niches. I have explained why high-demand products are the finest to sell. Now let's examine how to analyze product competition.

1. Use AMZ Suggestion Expander

AMZ Suggestion Expander aids in locating the competition and long-tail keywords for Amazon-hosted products. Using sophisticated data and analysis, AMZ Suggestion Expander also aids you in locating the best product to sell.

All the information you require is readily available, and you will never have trouble locating relevant results. AMZ Suggestion Expander provides you with all the information you need to run a successful business, as well as a list of the top-selling products on Amazon. AMZ Suggestion Expander is intended to provide the most precise and effective results.

I strongly suggest beginning your marketing research with the most well-known product in your niche. You will be able to monitor the products that are performing well on the market in this manner.

Here are the top Amazon products.

Home and Kitchen Appliances

Personal Care and Beauty Products

Toys and Children's Goods

Apparel & Footwear Gadgets

Bonus: Goal Wizard

As a thank you for reading this book, I'd like to provide you with a complimentary affiliate marketing resource I've created. The free tool is known as the Goal Wizard. I ordinarily charge $27 for access, but you have it for free because you are reading this book.

The Goal Wizard is a simple form, but once you've filled it out, the wizard will work his magic and help you break down your seemingly unattainable objectives into small, actionable steps.

The most difficult aspect of any objective is not knowing how to achieve it, because it seems so distant. Reverse-engineering your big goal into actionable actions to get you from where you are now to your goal is an effective strategy for overcoming this obstacle.

With affiliate marketing, your aim is likely to be able to quit your 9-to-5 job, make enough money to support yourself, your family, and go out with your friends, rather than being a hermit who always has to cancel social plans due to a lack of time or money. Actually, you should have an existence outside of work. Modern thought is absurd, but it is something we should all strive for.

To achieve this lofty objective, you must be aware of the sum of money required.

You cannot simply state, "Oh, I want to be wealthy so I can have more free time" or "I want to be wealthy so I can spend more time with my family and engage in hobbies," nor can you have an arbitrary quantity of wealth. You cannot claim, "Oh, I need a million dollars because that's how much money wealthy people have."

Everyone desires a million dollars, but you may not even need that much to live your ideal existence. If you have an expensive lifestyle, you may need more money, but you still need to know how much you need to attain your objective.

To determine this specific, lofty objective amount, you must list all of your expenses and the additional costs associated with an ideal lifestyle. Once you have a number, you can include it in your Big Goal using the Goal Wizard.

Now that you know your monthly financial goal, you can divide it into actionable actions.

Therefore, the first step is to break it down into two primary actions that will help you earn that quantity of money. In affiliate marketing, these steps may include creating a blog and a YouTube channel to promote the blog's content.

You cannot simply state, "I want a website" or "I want to start a blog"; you must further simplify these terms. You must break these down into "I need this much traffic on my website and this many ranking pages with this much keyword search volume to generate this much traffic." "I need this many YouTube subscribers. I probably need that many useful videos to acquire that many subscribers.

On the final level of goal decomposition, you need actual, small, tactical, and actionable actions that you can take.

How does one acquire subscribers? Perhaps you need to produce a video every week or every day.

How will you attract X number of visitors to your website in order to receive X number of views on your affiliate offer and earn X number of dollars? Well then, you must outline the steps you will follow.

In this instance, you are generating traffic via YouTube. But what other steps are necessary to generate this volume of traffic? Do you require instruction on how to rank YouTube videos? How will you conduct YouTube keyword research?

It is all about breaking down that seemingly unreachable and unattainable primary objective into actionable steps.

Because after completing this with the Goal Wizard, it will no longer appear to be an insurmountable objective.

It is extremely specific and measurable. And you will be able to make what you require materialize. Because you are aware of the next actions to take.

Chapter 7: How To Launch An Affiliate Marketing Campaign

Are you prepared to begin affiliate marketing? Here are a few suggestions to get you begun.

Select a reputable affiliate network. There are numerous networks available, but they are not all created equal. Conduct research to identify a company with a solid reputation and an extensive selection of products and services.

Select the appropriate products. Not every product is suitable for affiliate marketing. Conduct research and identify products that you believe in and that will appeal to your target audience.

Create quality content. This is essential for affiliate marketing success. If you want your readers to navigate through to the product page and make a purchase, you must create high-quality, valuable content.

Keyword Analysis

Prior to generating the content, we must have a list of profitable keywords to write about...

As a beginner, you must choose long-tail keywords so that you can begin earning money within months rather than years.

The subsequent video will provide you with all information regarding long-tail keywords. I hope, after watching the video, you have an understanding of what a long-tail term is, why it is important, how it operates, etc...

After several months of focusing on long-tail keywords, your site gains authority from Google and begins to rank for short-tail keywords as well.

Then you can also prioritize short-tail keywords.

Here, I will demonstrate the potential of a single keyword; however, this keyword is not a long-tail keyword; you can target these types of keywords after establishing authority and ranking. Therefore, I suggest beginning with long-tail keywords, followed by short-tail keywords.

The keyword is "MASSAGE CHAIR" and the monthly search volume is "49,000." According to a study, the No. 1 blog(website) on Google would receive "30% to 42%" of the visitors. However, if I could capture even 10% of the traffic on this site, I would receive nearly 4,900 visitors. The massage chair's price ranges from $750 to $9000, so I estimate the average price to be $1500. So let's investigate a modest calculation of revenue for this period below.

You have seen how a single word can alter the game. How profitable would you be if, after a few months of hard work on a blog, your site ranked for three to four keywords against stiff competition? However, remember that persistent and intelligent effort is always required.

SEMrush is the best keyword research tool in the industry, and the same tool is used in the video. Since there are so many restrictions on the free account, I recommend that you sign up for the 7-Day Free Trial instead. During the 7-day trial period, you can research and save enough keywords to create a blog. You may renew your coverage if you desire, but I believe 7 days is sufficient.

Chapter 8: How To Write An Email

Sure, you already know how to send emails; you do it every day. However, you're only writing to individuals you know, so you're rarely blocked by a spam filter. Writing business e-mails is a distinct bag of worms and requires some dexterity on your part to have them opened every time they arrive in someone's inbox.

What do you do immediately after checking your inbox? Check the email's header to see who sent it and what it says. How do you proceed if the title is uninteresting? Correct, you clicked the delete button. As an affiliate marketer, you desire your message to be opened and read.

How to Have Your Email Read

You have 50 characters including spaces available in the subject line. What you say will determine the success or failure of your next email campaign. The subject line should be captivating and draw their attention.

The best source for headline and subject line ideas is the local newspaper. Similar to newspaper headlines, the subject line of an email should inform the recipient of what to expect in the message. This may not work always. Such is reality. One campaign may explode in popularity while the next fizzles out. You can be assured of having more hits than mistakes with practice and a few pointers and suggestions.

Follow the first rule of email marketing to reduce the number of misses: TEST, TEST, TEST, and then TEST some more. You are experimenting with designs and trends that seem to work. Pick your subject line BEFORE you compose your body content. It must be the first step in every email marketing campaign. Then, conduct a test with your team and possibly a subset of your email contact lists.

Imagine you have a list of approximately 300 email addresses. Try out two alternative topic lines and record the results. How many responses did each heading receive? Then, modify one word and resend it to your list. This must be done consistently, as each email campaign will be unique by choice and necessity.

Keep track of the rate at which emails are examined. It's one thing for your email to be perused, but it's quite another for someone to respond or sign up. Even if you have a great subject line and your email is opened, it is a failure if it does not result in conversions.

The second rule of e-mail marketing is to personalize your subject lines, which means that one of the 50 words you have to work with should be the recipient's name. At least if the content and interests of the email are tailored to the prospects' interests. If it is a mass emailing, however, this does not apply.

The third tenet of email marketing is to always be honest. Do not delude your customers by promising more than the email can deliver. If your subject line does not accurately reflect the content of the message, your prospect will doubt you, and your email will be discarded.

The fourth rule of email marketing is to initiate a conversation. Without a conversation and a connection, you are sending a chilly email to a stranger.

Therefore, it will be more difficult for you to tell them about your company. It is dialogue if you send a series of emails to prospects and each one is a continuation of a discussion from a previous email.

The fifth rule of email marketing is to identify the email's sender to the recipient. Remember that you have 50 characters for the subject line, so merely include your name in the from line. Your subject line is the first thing they see, so it must grab their focus.

The content must be relevant to the subject line and engaging. Capable of compelling the reader to peruse the entire email. The body of your email must include a call to action that encourages recipients to do something, such as select a link or fill out a form.

Continue to send emails. You continue sending them until your prospect subscribes. Not everyone is prepared to participate when initially invited. If you have perseverance, they may eventually join you.

Chapter 9: Making Money Through Advertising

Email marketing

Targeting your current, former, and prospective consumers with email marketing are the three most important demographics. Create a database of their names and email addresses in a spreadsheet. If the email addresses are still required, collection must commence immediately. Use your website, storefront, front desk, and every phone call to solicit email addresses from visitors so you can begin developing your list.

If you cannot guarantee the confidentiality of their email addresses and other personal information, many individuals will be reluctant to join your email list. This should be guaranteed in advance. In addition to the initial vow, create a privacy statement that will be included at the bottom of every email you send. Be succinct in your response.

How to promote and generate transactions without cost

Include visitors to your website on your list of prospects because they are undoubtedly interested in your product or service. If a visitor leaves without registering or making a purchase, they are never identified again.

There is a superior strategy. By providing accurate contact information in real time, site monitoring software such as LeadLander allows you to convert unqualified visitors into qualified leads. Using the I.P. addresses of website visitors, you can compile a comprehensive database of prospective leads that includes business names, email addresses, telephone numbers, and even LinkedIn profiles. You can integrate it with your customer relationship management (CRM) system for simple lead scoring.

Although businesses frequently view social media as a tool for generating leads, it also helps to build brands. This is because social media sites like Facebook, Instagram, Twitter, LinkedIn, and YouTube contain so much information and so many people use them.

Website and social media channels are your first line of defense for acquiring free leads. Given that there are millions of blogs, websites, and social media pages to investigate, the need for a visually enticing layout is greater than ever. If your website's exit rate is high or your social media following is declining, you should update your website's appearance and navigation.

Affiliate passive revenue from blogging

The issue of blog monetization is complex. Although you can begin by offering services on your website, this is not passive income. When writing articles for a freelance client, you are compensated for your time.

No money begins to arrive. You must initially develop and implement multiple monetization strategies. When you employ a clever model and administer it routinely, you can generate passive income.

Chapter 10: Affiliate Marketing Comprehensively

You must understand the most commonly used terms in affiliate marketing. In fact, even the finest instructional classes can overlook this and will not (by any stretch of the imagination) adequately explain the various terms. Here is an alphabetical list of the most frequently used subsidiary marketing terms:

Promotion Restrictions

A promotion blocker is a piece of code that users enable in their browsers to prevent advertisements from displaying on websites. It is estimated that approximately 15% of Internet users have some form of advertisement blocker enabled, as the number of users of ad-blocking software has increased substantially over time.

Promotion barriers are terrible information for advertiser members. If your advertisement does not appear, you will not receive any commissions. Unfortunately, a large number of dishonest advertisers have contributed to the development of this innovation. There is currently no method to circumvent ad blocking.

Publicist

The best method to characterize a sponsor is as a business or individual seeking to promote their products or services. They are the product or service vendors. These sponsors understand that by selecting associates, they will increase the receptivity to their offers. A publicist pays commissions to subsidiaries for deals or potential efforts they bring.

Mission Division

A subsidiary mission is one in which you, as a partner, advance an item or assist a specific group. Frequently, the seller of a product or service will have a sales channel that you can promote. The vendor will pay you an agreed-upon commission for every transaction you close.

Associate missions are primarily focused on driving targeted traffic to a subsidiary offer. You can choose between free and paid member crusades:

a. Traffic from free virtual entertainment, web indexes, and other sources.

b. Paid traffic from web-based entertainment promotions or search engine marketing

Then, the ceiling is the limit. You can analyze the measurements of your member missions and then make adjustments, for instance to enhance transformation rates.

Subsidiary Exposure

A member exposure is an explanation you provide on your website to indicate that you are a partner for some of the products and services you promote. Here, you will inform site visitors that if they utilize your site's links to make a purchase, you may receive a commission.

The Federal Trade Commission (FTC) in the United States has mandated that all member advertisers must recall an offshoot disclosure for their website. Failure to comply may result in hefty penalties.

Partner Connection

Occasionally, a companion connection will be referred to as an offshoot ID or an external reference. When you become a partner for a product or service, your unique subsidiary connection distinguishes you from all other partners. This is essential for subsidiary organizations with a large number of collaborators.

The merchant should be able to correlate a transaction with you. Using an engaging offshoot interface is the optimal method for achieving this goal. Typically, when pursuing a partner program, you will be asked to provide a unique username. Then, this is incorporated into your exceptional member joins.

Your one-of-a-kind affiliation with a subsidiary is essential to your incentives. You would prefer not to exert a great deal of effort promoting a product or service only to have your business licensed to a competitor! Today, offshoot initiatives and organizations have a feature that allows you to automatically replicate your unique member connection. Ensure that you use this effectively.

Chapter 11: Ppc Marketing And Other Promotional Methods

Nevertheless, consider a situation in which you do not have a group of individuals. Imagine a scenario in which you are not a force to be reckoned with and have not earned your readers' trust. In this situation, you should find direct methods of sending visitors to your specials page. Facebook and AdWords are effective PPC (Pay Per Click) platforms for accomplishing this. PPC indicates that you may pay when someone actually clicks on your ad. You determine your maximum "per-click" expenditure and the financial plan's endpoint. If you set your cost per click too low, your advertisement will not appear if there are numerous competing advertisements from competing firms in the same industry. If you set it too high, you will likely lose money.

When posting promotions on Facebook, you'll want to limit who sees your clients' identities based on the information they share with the social network. These include: Age Gender Location Recreational activities and interests Job Title Salary Others' interests

This is only the beginning!

When placing advertisements on Google through AdWords, it is important to consider not only the individual's interests (based on what they are searching for - the "keywords"), but also their expectations. Aim is a crucial aspect of pay-per-click (PPC) advertising, as it reveals whether a user is merely looking or intending to purchase. If they are investigating, they could search for "best PC games of this year." If they are interested in purchasing, they could then search for the PC game's name or "modest PC games." You can also use "negative catchphrases" to exclude phrases that could imply someone is not interested in purchasing and therefore has an objectionable plan (such as "free download").

The purpose of pay-per-click advertising is to ensure that people ONLY click on your link if they are likely to purchase from you. This reduces the amount spent while increasing the anticipated benefit. This necessitates that the advertisements be as "targeted" as possible, even if it scares away people who aren't likely to be interested in purchasing using the appropriate keywords. The link should clearly direct users to a specials page in order to maximize your profits. Then, you must zero in on your website's rate of change. In other words, if your landing page is well-written, it may convert one percent of visitors (meaning one percent of visitors purchase your product). The higher this number, the more advertising you can afford to spend while still turning a profit.

Direct Marketing Via Facebook and Other Platforms

You can also sell directly through these other platforms, of course. There is nothing preventing you from sharing an affiliate link with your Facebook group or Instagram (in your bio or once the swipe up feature is available on stories). If you don't have the skills or time to create a website, this is a good method to build an engaged audience.

OWN YOUR RELATIONSHIP WITH YOUR AUDIENCE:

Take responsibility for your relationship with your audience. The key to making money as an affiliate marketer is to have a loyal audience that is interested in what you have to say. This is difficult to accomplish if your content marketing campaigns struggle to reach them.

Affiliate marketers who wish to share their product recommendations frequently utilize social media and YouTube channels as their first port of call. However, reliance on these online channels is hazardous for a number of reasons.

Mitigate this risk and establish a direct communication channel with your audience by inviting them to join an email list. In addition to having complete control over how and when your affiliate content reaches your audience, you also arrive in a space that is not oversaturated: their inbox.

This affiliate marketing suggestion need not be complex. Simply add a pop-up box to your website that offers a complimentary checklist or discount code in exchange for newsletter subscription.

4: Know the product you are recommending inside and out:

Sadly, affiliate marketing has made its way into nearly every "get rich quick" scheme. This is accompanied by a deluge of people who are only interested in making money and not in authentically assisting their audience. Those individuals typically fail quickly.

Mark Valderrama, CEO and co-founder of Aquarium Store Depot, asserts, "You can distinguish yourself from the competition by having more knowledge than they do." "In order to stand out as an affiliate, you must be recognized as an expert or have a website where people can learn more about the products you're promoting." It is all too common for affiliates to select a handful of providers they believe will be of interest to their visitors without conducting any background research. However, even if you are only seeking information about these items, you are still interested in how and why people use them.

To accomplish this, Mark advises you to "perform your due diligence prior to signing up with a new service provider. Consider the opinions of others before attempting it yourself, even if it's a trial version." Although it may take longer to generate sales for your affiliate products, once you do, individuals will be more likely to trust the products you recommend.

Best Methods for Writing Product Evaluations

This implies that instead of providing only surface-level information, you should share any first-hand insights you have and not be afraid to delve into a product's flaws.

This will make the content appear objective and demonstrate that you have actual experience with the product.

Other effective affiliate content types include comparison and summary articles.

The Top Posts

Roundup entries list multiple solutions for a particular use case. Essentially, they are less in-depth product evaluations for multiple products at once. You can also consider these to be "Best" postings, as their titles are typically "15 Best Tools for" Here is an example of a post that compares the most effective social media marketing tools.

Illustrations of Affiliate Marketing Posts;

Product Comparison Articles

As the term implies, comparisons compare two (or more) distinct products. For instance, if you're an affiliate in the web hosting niche, you could compose a "Bluehost vs. Kinsta" comparison.

Find out more

Our affiliate marketing course contains all the information necessary for creating content for a website devoted to affiliate marketing.

Google provides targeted traffic.

As you add high-quality content to your website, you'll need to devise a plan to entice visitors to select your affiliate links and ultimately make purchases.

There are multiple methods to attract visitors to a website. The most effective of these traffic sources is search engine traffic from Google and other engines.

Google traffic is so valuable because it allows you to target an extremely specific group of individuals.

You cannot afford to have random or disinterested visitors on your site if you want to make money.

Using Google Search, you can create content that targets individuals who are interested in your products because you know exactly what they are looking for.

Remember that not all keywords are identical. While you should target search terms with a high search volume, you should also ensure that the keywords have purchase intent and are not simply general queries.

For instance, a user who conducts a search for "what is a web hosting platform?" is likely inquisitive and not ready to purchase.

You should concentrate on keywords with commercial and transactional intent.

Contextual connections

The majority of your placements of affiliate links will consist of contextual links. These are URL connections that have been placed within the body of your content.

The optimal location for these links will vary depending on the type of article you are composing. In a product review, for instance, you can add an affiliate link to the first mention of the product name.

Illustration of a Contextual Link.

For a comparison listicle analyzing ten distinct products, you can add an affiliate link to each product's header.

If the content is a promotional post, you can also consider including a more direct call to action (CTA) with the link.

Banners

In general, contextual links are the most effective for increasing sales, but it can be beneficial to include other forms of links as well.

Banners allow you to add visually enticing graphics that attract the attention of site visitors. You can position them in the sidebar or the body of your posts.

Numerous affiliate programs include banners and other marketing materials, so you don't have to design them yourself.

Resources page

A resources page displays a list of pertinent tools for your target audience. After establishing yourself as an authority in your industry, these pages can be an effective means of directing readers to your affiliate offers.

You may include your affiliate link and a concise description of what each tool does and why you recommend it for each.

Email

Include your affiliate links in your email marketing messages for an additional effective use of them.

You should apply the same principle to your email marketing campaigns by combining informative and promotional messages.

Add an email subscription to your website and begin sending subscribers regular emails. Similar to the content you post, the more valuable information you provide in these messages, the more trust you will earn from your audience.

Once you've earned your subscribers' trust, you can send them the occasional affiliate marketing message.

Consider Employing a Link Management Platform

Use an affiliate link management platform as a final tip. As you sign up for multiple affiliate programs, you will require a method for efficiently organizing and keeping track of all your connections.

A plugin for affiliate links will provide a central location for storing links, and you can easily view statistics to determine which links are receiving the most clicks.

Again, promoting high-paying products is essential to achieving this revenue target. If you were promoting low-paying items, it would require a significant amount of time to acquire the necessary traffic.

Chapter 12: The Idea Behind Drop Shipping

You have an online store from which you sell products, but none of these items are stored in your warehouse or at your residence.

When a customer places an order through your Drop shipping store, you place a corresponding order with your Drop shipping provider. Don't fret. There are numerous applications available to help automate this procedure.

The remainder will be managed by your Drop shipping provider. Consider packing and shipping the order directly to the consumer.

Your customer will now receive the delivery directly from your Drop shipping provider, without you ever touching the merchandise!

The most frequently asked question today is, "Will my customer notice that the delivery did not come from me?"

Is there no advertising or recipe from the source, for instance, on the packaging?

No.

You must ensure that your supplier is willing to facilitate both Drop shipping and blind Drop shipping.

Blind Drop shipping entails ensuring that no aspect of the cargo to the customer could lead them to suspect that you are Drop shipping. No advertisements or invoices from your Drop shipping provider, for instance! Your customers will simply obtain the products without being aware that you are drop shipping!

The following is an example of a common business strategy that does not utilize a drop shipper:

In order to obtain a wholesale price, your company routinely orders products from a supplier, typically in Minimum Order Quantities (MOQs).

Your company will store the goods until a consumer places an order.

You process, package, and ship each and every order directly to the consumer.

Using a Drop shipper modifies the procedure marginally:

A client submits an order with your business.

You communicate the order information to your Drop shipper.

It is typical for Drop transporters to charge a wholesale price for the product they are selling in addition to a Drop shipping fee.

The merchandise is then packaged and dispatched to the customer. You are not responsible for storing or packaging the products.

In a nutshell, drop shipping is the practice of marketing a product through your website without being responsible for its actual fulfillment and shipping. Another significant benefit of Drop shipping is that you do not pay for the product until the client does, making it an attractive option for those who do not want to spend a lot of money on initial inventory or who do not want to take a chance on purchasing items that will not sell. With such a low barrier to entry, anyone, from absolute beginners to seasoned business owners, can launch their own Drop shipping eCommerce business.

Does this suggest that the Drop shipping business model is suitable for you? The response will vary based on your objectives and talent set. Let's first examine the advantages and disadvantages of Drop shipping.

Chapter 13: What Is Dropshipping

Dropshipping is a type of e-commerce business strategy that differs from conventional e-commerce in that you do not physically handle or store the products you sell. You can build your own website for your online store, or you can utilize services such as Shopify, Amazon, or eBay.

You offer customers a range of products sourced from reputable manufacturers and wholesalers who specialize in your market segment. The domino effect begins when your client places an order with you.

Your order is received by your supplier. After billing you for the agreed-upon amount, your supplier dispatches the merchandise directly to your customer.

Your suppliers may be located anywhere in the world, depending on the specific items you sell. There are no restrictions on the location of your suppliers, and this also applies to delicate products. Because inventory is not sitting on the shelf waiting to be sold before its expiration date, the time required to produce and ship a product to a customer is reduced.

When you choose to launch a business based on the dropshipping business model, it radically alters how you conduct business and provides your company with a great deal of operational flexibility.

How Does It Operate?

With dropshipping, a business can take advantage of all the benefits of selling without the burdens of stocktaking and inventory costs. You won't need thousands of dollars' worth of materials to get started because you never own the items you sell. In addition, you will no longer be responsible for the expensive insurance, security, and maintenance costs associated with the actual inventory on your shelves.

Obviously, you do not need a physical location to operate your business, as customers will never need to physically visit your location to make a purchase. Dropshipping requires only a computer, an internet connection, and occasionally a workstation to get started.

Cons and Advantages

Compared to traditional retail operations, outsourcing offers several advantages. However, there are numerous obstacles that make it difficult to begin.

Pros

Low start-up expenses: The first and most obvious advantage of dropshipping is that it is inexpensive to get begun. Everything about dropshipping is designed to take advantage of the Internet and provide you with a straightforward, stress-free, and profitable investment opportunity.

Low-cost inventory: Dropshipping does more than allow you to launch your business with the cheapest inventory. In addition, it allows you to open your "shop" with no inventory! Once consumers are located, suppliers and delivery companies will manage the remainder of the process. There is no reason to get your hands soiled.

Low cost of order fulfillment Order fulfillment is the most expensive aspect of online businesses. Before the goods can be loaded into a delivery vehicle or bicycle, online retailers must perform the laborious duties of warehousing, monitoring, labeling, packaging, and ultimately transportation. Each of these services' costs are accounted for in a dropshipping transaction. The supplier commission and delivery service charge are added to the price paid by the consumer. You compete with other dropshippers for the limited number of consumers and establish your own margin.

Lower risk of loss: Since dropshipping does not require any inventory or physical space, the risk of losing money is quite low. In actuality, the only upfront costs associated with dropshipping are the advertising costs required to promote your business. Since the foundation will already exist, you can ride the surge and spend significantly less on advertising by selecting items that are already performing well among other dropshippers.

Cons

Having no control over the procedure: The disadvantage of outsourcing order fulfillment and client delivery is that you have little control over either. Even if you have little control over the situation and can do nothing about it, their mistakes will reflect negatively on you.

Reduced profits: When they purchase inventory, conventional merchants receive discounts due to their mass purchases. Consequently, their profit margins are greater. In dropshipping, the margin you can apply to a product and still make money is relatively low.

Therefore, in order to generate the same quantity of profit as traditional retailers, you must sell more products.

To make dropshipping work, you must simultaneously manage the connections between the supplier and the customer, according to many. If the supplier delivers the incorrect product, damages the items, or is late in fulfilling the order, the customer will criticize you for a circumstance over which you had little control. When you communicate with clients and vendors via phone, text message, or email, you forfeit the opportunity to establish a human connection.

Budget: The budgetary requirements for launching a dropshipping business on Shopify include the costs of establishing a website, a merchant account with Shopify, shop improvements to better your selling platform, and marketing your company to attract customers.

In order to establish a dropshipping business on Shopify, you must first register a premium account. The least expensive plan costs $29 per month and includes unlimited items, two staff accounts, 24/7 support, and support for hardware peripherals. For an additional $50, you can receive five staff accounts, gift cards, expert report creators, and a $0.02 discount on in-person credit card rates. The first 14 days are free so that you can determine if you wish to continue with the paid plan.

Next on the list is purchasing a domain name for your online store. A dropshipping website must be deftly crafted and adhere to the stringent standards of e-commerce websites. $14 is all that's required to acquire a domain via Shopify. To assist with this, you can open an Oberlo dropshipping app for $29, which gives you access to AliExpress as well. Spocket is an excellent instrument that connects you with dropshipping suppliers from all over the world. If you wish to add more than 24 products to your store, you must convert to a premium account.

Investing in store enhancements can increase sales and profits. You cannot add bulk discounts, sale pop-ups, cross-selling, or countdown timers to a standard Shopify account. These enhancements cost between $19 and $30 each, but will significantly increase your store's profitability. Due to their greater importance, you may choose to begin with the discounted pop-ups ($19) and sales pop-ups (free). If you have a limited budget to begin with, you can add additional items as you go.

Marketing is the scourge of any organization. According to marketers, even the world's finest product would not outsell the worst if it had superior marketing. In dropshipping, the initial phases of a business are crucial. Without advertising, you will not be able to attract the first customers who will establish your shop's reputation. Contact a highly targeted audience using Google or Facebook advertisements, which are the most effective, for maximum impact. Daily expenses of $5 to $10 should suffice. The amount increases to approximately $105 when a reserve for the first two weeks is included (when dropshippers typically begin to generate revenue). However, the product is in high demand, so it may never reach this extent. By the end of the second week, you will likely be earning a substantial profit and using that money to market your business.

If you utilize Shopify's 14-day free trial and Oberlo's premium service for your store, the total cost of starting a dropshipping business is approximately $200. If you choose the Shopify free service and the free Spocket bundle, the total cost is approximately $170. In any event, marketing incurs the greatest expenses. This is very reasonable, given that if you don't market your business, you probably won't acquire any customers. Instead of believing the nonsense that there are no initial costs in certain locations, it is more prudent to commit to the process and risk failure than to believe the folly. If you genuinely desire it, the risk is unquestionably worthwhile.

9. Mindset: If you lack the proper mindset, you cannot succeed in anything. Everyone has undoubtedly heard this expression at some point. The same applies to drop shipment. As a dropshipper, you won't get very far if you don't take the time to cultivate the right attitude. You inquire what kind of mentality it is. As a dropshipper, you must have an entrepreneurial mindset in order to succeed. Entrepreneurs now rule the globe because they initially sought to do so. They accomplish this by fostering subsequent attitudes.

Numerous obstacles encountered on the business path can intimidate individuals into inaction. You decide that you must first develop the best feasible business strategy. Because of a dread of failure, you continually alter the company's strategy, which costs you the opportunity. The research trap, on the other hand, occurs when you decide to gather as much information as possible about a topic before commencing. You will eventually discover information that convinces you it would be ridiculous to even begin. You ultimately concede and initiate development of the subsequent concept. The action mentality suggests acquiring only the necessary information and proceeding with the plan. What fails can always be rectified in the future.

A fixation on financial flow Cash flow is the essence of any business. You cannot survive for more than a few months without money. Consider how every action you take for the company and every dollar you invest will contribute to the company's revenue generation. If you cannot acquire paying customers, you will eventually be forced to close your business.

You must be open to change, willing to make adjustments, and adaptable to novel circumstances. If something about your dropshipping business isn't working, don't be hesitant to change it as long as you stay on track. For example, after a few days of advertising, a larger group of Japanese anime fans approaches you and asks if you carry a particular product. You had initially targeted Manga comics consumers. You don't say that I sell Manga comics and merchandise. Instead, you find a supplier of Japanese anime merchandise and alter your audience.

Every successful entrepreneur has a substantial history of failure as their foundation. They stand out from the throng because they attempt after each failure and instead of giving up, they make adjustments. If your initial dropshipping endeavor fails, attempt a new product or strategy and you'll soon be celebrating with the best.

Developing a Store

If you are selling multiple affiliate products, you can establish a store to sell them from, which is also a very effective strategy. This means that, similar to an e-commerce website, you will emphasize and promote products that are relevant to your brand. The only significant distinction is that when a customer clicks on your item, they will now be redirected to an external page.

This is simple to accomplish; for instance, you could use WooCommerce, an e-commerce plugin compatible with WordPress. This will allow you to create a store on your website for visitors to peruse products. It allows affiliate links, so anyone who clicks on a product will be redirected to the new website.

Multiple Methods to Sell

However, what about incorporating hyperlinks directly into your articles? This is a fantastic method to monetize a website or blog, even though very few affiliates utilize it. Include an affiliate link within the article's body, then write about any subject that interests you. This allows you to subtly advertise the product, and anyone interested in your content can click on the link.

Similar to adding AdSense to your website, but you actively encourage visitors to select the link and earn a much larger reward. Even acknowledge that it generates income if you so choose!

In many countries around the world, it is required by law that you report any profits made from these products.

Use a plugin to automatically add a note to the bottom of each page on your website, but don't neglect!

One of the best content formats for promoting affiliate products is a top ten list. If you work in the fitness industry, you could compile a list of the best home gym equipment, and if you write about technology, you could discuss the most powerful laptops on the market today.

Whatever you want to accomplish, this will work well for clicks and revenue and lend itself to rich snippets, which can make it stand out substantially in the search engine results pages (SERPs) for your content.

Similarly, there is nothing preventing you from including an affiliate link in the message body.

This is an excellent method for reaching individuals directly in their inbox when they may be receptive to your offers.

eBooks can contain affiliate links as well. If you're selling or giving away a digital product, you can include URLs to your PDF. Those who are perusing this are likely very interested in your brand and will therefore likely purchase what you recommend. Since these are qualified leads, the context is optimal for attempting to sell even more expensive products.

What if you could sell a digital product for $20 per unit and earn a ton more money from those who read your book and follow your advice?

Printing an affiliate link on a brochure or leaflet is another option. Using a URL that is simple and easy to remember is the easiest way to use this.

It redirects the user to your affiliate link. Thus, you can advertise your products in person!

These recommendations are intended to demonstrate that you do not always need to aggressively pitch your product; rather, you can attempt a soft sell by simply including a link, possibly with an image.

This is very effective for tangible products (especially if you use a well-designed button and the item is actively related to the page's content). Simply incorporating buy links into your content could result in a number of transactions, which could add up if you have a successful website with a large audience and plenty of content.

You need only be creative to use affiliate links in a variety of alternative methods. Try new things and conduct tests to determine what works best for you and your product. You might be amazed!

Chapter 14: Real-World Examples Of Superb Affiliate Marketing Success

Observing affiliate marketers who have achieved great success is one of the best methods to learn how to do it yourself. Instead of purchasing their products, which is also a good notion, you could investigate their operations.

Below are a few concise case studies of two well-known elite affiliates. The next time you decide to offer affiliate products, you should be able to learn a few things by reading these case studies and observing their behavior attentively.

Stephen Fox

If you are unfamiliar with Andrew Fox, you should maintain a close eye on him and pay him close attention. In the near future, he will be a ubiquitous name in internet marketing. In 2002, at the age of 21 and with only a high school diploma, he was requested to speak at the Internet Super Conference.

He was by far the youngest speaker to accept the award. He was nevertheless able to attain success in his field despite his advanced age and lack of a graduate degree. It is not necessary to be an expert in a particular subject to be a successful affiliate marketer, so anyone who queries their qualifications should be aware of this.

Some of Andrew's enormously successful businesses have nothing to do with internet marketing. For example, he created a dating and messaging website for the United Kingdom.

In addition to selling his own products, Andrew is also an affiliate for a number of other companies. His monthly earnings have reportedly reached $46,000, but he had to work up to 16 to 18 hours per day, including vacations and holidays, to get to this point. Consequently, you may need to exert a great deal of effort if you wish to achieve the same level of success as Andrew.

The Jeremy Chia

Presently, Ewen Chia is a maestro of internet marketing. I must inform you this, however. You have probably already heard of him. There is a good chance that you have already purchased one of his numerous high-quality Internet marketing informational products.

You may be unaware of Ewen Chia's remarkable success as an affiliate marketer. Gently is, or was for many years, the "number one affiliate marketer in the world," according to many Internet marketing experts.

In contrast to the majority of affiliate marketers, Ewen does not employ five-year-old strategies. Rather, if you peruse any of the sales pages for his affiliate marketing products, you're likely to discover strategies you've never seen before.

In his affiliate marketing classes, Ewen teaches students, for instance, how to showcase websites for free on CNN, Google, Yahoo, and other prominent websites. He also demonstrates how to generate traffic without using conventional techniques such as PPC, SEO, or Web 2.0 workarounds.

Ewen also employs and teaches the following techniques to entice visitors who will purchase affiliate products:

Using "ethical bribes" on Myspace; placing products in hot marketplaces that 99 percent of marketers are oblivious of; tricking people into unwittingly promoting your affiliate products on eBay; and using "lost sites" to drive traffic.

Ewen employs and promotes strategies that are anything but common or mundane. Most of them are likely items that you have never used. I recommend paying strict attention to him in order to learn more about affiliate marketing.

Chapter 15: Some Certain Methods To Immediately Boost Your Affiliate Income

In a perfect affiliate marketing world, you would not be responsible for constructing and maintaining your own website, handling customer service and refunds, or developing new products. This is a straightforward and effective method for earning money online immediately. What actions would you take if you are already enrolled in an affiliate program? Shouldn't the commissions be multiplied or even tripled? What is the secret? With these tried-and-true methods, you can instantly double or even triple the profits of your affiliate program.

Determine which products and initiatives will generate the most revenue. Clearly, you must promote a program that enables you to earn the most money in the shortest amount of time. The selection of such software is confounded by a number of factors. Choose the ones with the greatest commissions. Ensure that your products are a suitable fit for your niche market. In addition to a company that has a track record of promptly and readily compensating its affiliates. If you want to expand your portfolio, you should abandon a program that isn't producing results. There are hundreds of affiliate programs available online, so you can be selective. For the sake of your marketing budget, you should presumably choose the best option. Create and distribute brief ebooks or complimentary reports on your website. As an affiliate, you will likely face competition from others marketing the same program. Writing concise reports about the product you are marketing is an excellent way to differentiate yourself from the competition and acquire a loyal following. Include some gratis recommendations in the reports. Include product recommendations if possible. E-books are a dependable source of data. Customers will observe this, and it will increase the likelihood that they will give you a shot.

When individuals register for your free publications, be sure to collect their email addresses. It is common knowledge that people do not purchase when accosted for the first time with the intent of making a purchase. It may be necessary to transmit your message more than six times if you want to make a sale. It is essential to keep track of who downloads your reports and publications for this reason alone. After making initial contact, you may send these contacts a reminder to purchase from you. Before directing a prospective client to a vendor's website, you should obtain some fundamental information from them. Consider that you are providing the product's creators with free publicity. Only when a sale is made will you receive payment. Sending prospective clients directly to the suppliers is a surefire way to loose them as clients. Once you have their contact information, you can send them additional marketing materials and receive payment for each message they open, not just for the initial sale. Create an electronic magazine. It is considerably simpler to sell something to a friend or relative than to a complete stranger. Due to this, you should initiate your own newsletter. In addition, this helps you establish credibility with your audience. This approach walks a fine line between useful information and overt salesmanship. By consistently publishing insightful editorials, you will cultivate reader loyalty, which may lead to increased sales.

Demand a larger-than-average percentage of sales from local businesses. If a particular promotion has been very successful, you may ask the store proprietor for a portion of the profits. If the store owner is wise, he or she will oblige with your request rather than risk losing a valuable customer like you. Your merchant cannot lose money on you, so do not be shy about requesting a commission increase. If possible, simply endeavor to see things from a more rational standpoint.

Create persuasive pay-per-click advertisements. The most effective form of Internet advertising is pay-per-click (PPC) search engines. Affiliates may generate income by managing pay-per-click (PPC) campaigns with Google AdWords and Overture. Then, monitor them to determine which advertisements are effective and which should be eliminated. Even a brief trial of these techniques may result in a significant increase in your commissions.

Finding a profitable niche should be your top priority if you wish to participate in affiliate marketing. Selecting a distinct niche market facilitates connections with advertisers and benefactors. Additionally, it focuses your marketing efforts and allows you to rapidly expand your audience.

When novice affiliate marketers begin their search for a niche, they frequently believe that they must locate a little-known market, or that profitable niches will be those in which few other marketers are involved. After all, the most popular industries and topics are dominated by established publications that invest substantial quantities of money each month in content creation, outreach, and SEO. For example, websites like Healthline and WebMD have the marketing budgets to employ freelance writers to create health-related content. In addition, they invest thousands of dollars in link building, paid promotions, and other forms of advertising. It goes without saying that it would be unfeasible for the average marketer to compete with these brands.

In spite of this, the finest market niches to target are the mainstream ones. These marketing niches have competition, high demand, demonstrated longevity, an abundance of discoverable consumers, and an abundance of related products, social media groups, forums, and websites. In the unlikely event that you discover a niche that other affiliate marketers have disregarded, it will be because demand is low – so there are few customers – and the number of products available for promotion is limited. That would be difficult for an experienced marketer, let alone a novice.

Focusing on an industry sub-niche such as 'health tips for seniors' or 'healthy living for families' can help you create a successful website and stand out from the competition. Thus, you can use long-tail keywords, which are ignored by larger publications, to generate search engine traffic and affiliate sales for your website. This is the more prudent course of action, since the niche is perpetual and you already know there are profits to be made. Here are seven simple methods for locating a profitable niche for affiliate marketing.

3. Evaluate the niche's level of competition and search volume

As previously stated, sectors with little competition should be avoided, as this typically indicates a limited profit potential. It is essential not to conflate niche analysis with keyword research, as this is a common error. You want to discover phrases with low to moderate competition when researching keywords, as you are attempting to rank highly for them. In contrast, the objective of niche analysis is to determine whether the niche itself is profitable.

SEMrush is an excellent starting point for your investigation. This tool does two things when you enter the broad keyword for your market niche. First, it displays dozens of additional keywords associated with your niche that can aid in your research. Secondly, it displays the keyword's difficulty, cost-per-click, and search volume. The keyword difficulty (KD) exposes how difficult it is to rank for a particular keyword, based on the authority of the websites currently occupying the top ten search results. Cost per click (CPC) indicates the average amount of money that marketers are willing to pay for a single click on a keyword. The search volume indicates how frequently a keyword is entered into Google.

Ideally, you should seek out keywords in your niche with a CPC of at least $2 and a search volume of at least 10,000. This indicates that the topic is sufficiently popular to generate substantial returns, and that advertisers are willing to pay a reasonable sum to have their ads displayed for these search terms. If many of the most important keywords in your niche have a high CPC, you can be confident that there are opportunities for profit. Marketers who pay several dollars per view without a guarantee of a sale must be making a fortune. Obtaining high rankings for these keywords in Google's organic search results is, of course, an additional challenge.

4. Determine the number of available traffic sources.

This step's significance cannot be overstated. You must determine if your niche has a variety of traffic sources, as this is essential for the sustainability of your online business. The best method to determine this is to examine the traffic sources of the top websites in your proposed niche. SimilarWeb is a useful resource for investigating the traffic origins of various websites. Determine if the best websites only receive traffic from search engines or if social media users are also accessing them. If the proportion of social media visitors is considerable, identify the networks from which they originate. In certain sectors, for example, the most popular websites receive a significant number of visitors from Instagram and Pinterest. The majority of these sites publish numerous images.

In fact, research indicates that only 31% of blog posts are discovered through search engines. The remaining customers are found through referrals, email lists, social networks, etc. Conduct a Facebook search to identify Facebook Groups that cater to your audience's interests. After conducting a keyword search for your niche, select the Groups icon to view the relevant communities. If your niche has active groups, you can attract visitors to your website by participating in these groups and publishing relevant content. There is nothing preventing you from creating and developing your own Facebook group.

YouTube is the second largest search engine in the world, so it makes sense to check if your prospects are active there. It takes time to develop a YouTube channel, but many highly trafficked topics and keywords are within reach due to the difficulty of video creation. If you do not use this platform immediately, you should at least keep it in mind for the future. Additionally, discussion websites like Reddit and forums can be effective traffic sources. Check to see if any conversations related to your niche are taking place on these sites. If they are, this is another possible source of traffic. Priority number one, however, should be determining how to develop a list of enthusiastic email subscribers so you can send website visitors on demand.

These are all crucial concerns to address, as a niche affiliate website with limited traffic sources typically has limited expansion potential. In all likelihood, search engine traffic will be your primary traffic source, but you should also consider other options to build a low-risk, sustainable enterprise. Competent affiliate marketers do not rely on a single traffic source.

5. Look for Market Gaps That You Can Exploit

To profit from the niche you pursue, you must offer superior website content compared to other websites in the niche. To accomplish this, you must identify the weaknesses in the content produced by your competitors and devise methods for improving it. First, peruse the content published by the leading websites in your industry and make a list of any issues. Then, contemplate how you can improve your performance. For instance, you could include more videos, GIFs, or images to distinguish your content from that of your competitors. Alternatively, you could make the content more comprehensive by incorporating case studies and specific examples.

In addition, there may be pressing issues regarding a topic that the leading websites fail to address. Reading the blog comments on these websites is a useful way to identify such omissions. The negative reviews of niche-related books on Amazon can provide insight into the type of content your audience desires to read.

Look for Market Weaknesses You Can Exploit.

To profit from the niche you pursue, you must offer superior website content compared to other websites in the niche.

To accomplish this, you must identify the weaknesses in the content produced by your competitors and devise methods for improving it. First, peruse the content published by the leading websites in your industry and make a list of any issues. Then, contemplate how you can improve your performance. For instance, you could include more videos, GIFs, or images to distinguish your content from that of your competitors. Alternatively, you could make the content more comprehensive by incorporating case studies and specific examples.

In addition, there may be pressing issues regarding a topic that the leading websites fail to address. Reading the blog comments on these websites is a useful way to identify such omissions. The negative reviews of niche-related books on Amazon can provide insight into the type of content your audience desires to read.

6) Investigate Previously Sold Websites and Profitable Acquisitions

The number of successful enterprises or websites in a niche is a reasonably reliable indicator of its value. Regular purchases of eCommerce stores, blogs, and other websites in your niche indicate there is profit potential. To discover this, visit the massive website marketplace Flippa and conduct a search for the primary keyword in your niche, such as "muscle building."

To view the profits of various websites, filter the results by 'Monthly Profit' and set the minimum quantity to $1,000 per month. Select 'ClickBank' and 'Amazon' from the 'Monetization' drop-down menu if you are only interested in sites that generate revenue through affiliate marketing. After clicking the 'search' icon, a selection of auctioned websites on Flippa will be displayed. If desired, the results can be sorted from highest to lowest price. Here, you can observe the performance statistics of websites and analyze their success. You can also identify areas for development that could contribute to the expansion of the websites.

This data can be extremely beneficial to your niche research because it exposes the various niches that people are entering in order to earn enormous amounts of money. You will be astounded by the amount of money that can be made in the most peculiar niches. Be mindful to record any brilliant ideas you encounter. Search for personally appealing websites that sold for a high price. If someone else can create a profitable niche website and sell it for a large quantity, there's no reason you can't do the same.

Empire Flippers is another good location to look for websites and online businesses for sale. This website features a marketplace where you can search for niche-specific keywords and filter the results to view recently sold businesses and websites. Empire Flippers displays the selling price and monthly profits of these websites without disclosing their addresses. Additionally, by tapping on a listing, you can view a wealth of information about a website, including its monthly visitors, income figures, target niche, and sources of income/traffic, etc. The evaluation of this data will reveal precisely how much various websites in your industry are earning and how quickly you can replicate their success.

7) Determine What Your Unique Selling Proposition Is

One final consideration must be made before settling on a particular niche for your affiliate website. What will be your unique perspective? How will you distinguish your website from the innumerable others available online? How do you ensure that people remember you? This issue is especially relevant in sectors with a great deal of competition.

Try to create a relatable narrative that piques your website visitors' interest. In the'make money online' niche, for instance, there are thousands of websites, but MyWifeQuitHerJob resonates with people more than most others due to its owner's backstory. The same can be said about SmartBlogger, another top website in this niche with an engaging narrative that attracts visitors.

You can also distinguish your website by making it more visually appealing or by becoming an authority in a subcategory of your niche. Brian Dean, the founder of Backlinko, was a late entrant to the SEO niche, but he transformed Backlinko into a leading SEO resource by producing highly insightful content. Comparatively, BestReviews towers head and shoulders above other review websites due to the company's rigorous testing of products prior to publishing reviews. Therefore, their readers have more faith in their reviews than in those of a typical affiliate website that publishes generic reviews with minimal research.

In one way or another, you must distinguish yourself from the throng by developing a distinct identity. The niche you select should lend itself naturally to this procedure. This will increase the likelihood that your audience will purchase the promoted products.

How to Locate a Profitable Niche – Conclusions

As an affiliate, it is your responsibility to identify profitable niches, determine whether they are worth entering, and then create high-quality content that addresses the problems of your prospects and establishes you as a reliable authority. Hopefully, you have realized by now that this is not as difficult as many people believe. Remember that there is no such thing as a 'saturated niche'. Profits can always be generated by adopting an innovative approach or simply outperforming the competition. Instead of feeling intimidated, simply roll up your sleeves, observe the above advice, and begin your search for a profitable niche today. There is no doubt that a lucrative affiliate niche is close at hand.

www.ingramcontent.com/pod-product-compliance
Lightning Source LLC
Chambersburg PA
CBHW050250120526
44590CB00016B/2287